December's Gift
An Interfaith Holiday Story

Written by Ashley Smith-Santos and Stasie Bitton
Illustrated by Sandra Salsbury

CRUNCH! Clara's bright-yellow boots made prints in the freshly fallen snow. She dug her hand deep into her pocket, touching the chocolate gelt. It was the first night of Chanukah! Clara would help cook the potato latkes with her grandmother Bubbe. She licked her lips. She could already taste the salty, crispy latke in her mouth.

Clara climbed aboard the train and settled in for the ride to her grandparents' house. Mittens pounced onto her lap and nuzzled his cold nose into her hand.

"Mittens! That's my dreidel!"

Running her fingers over each Hebrew letter, Clara remembered the rules of the game. Nun, Gimel, Hay, Shin, "a great miracle happened there." She couldn't wait to play again with PopPop.

"Shalom! Happy Chanukah!" Bubbe greeted Clara at the front door with a big hug and wrapped a soft scarf around her neck. "I knitted this especially for you," she cheerfully sang.

"Thank you, thank you!" Clara giggled as Mittens pawed at the fringe on the scarf. Clara breathed in the delicious, familiar aroma floating from Bubbe's kitchen.

"Let's cook!" Clara said and followed Bubbe into the kitchen.

Mittens peered into the mixing bowl, his whiskers darting back and forth as his blue eyes followed the whirl and swirl of yellow eggs. Clara and Bubbe laughed as the silver loops went around and around. Clara sprinkled a pinch of salt and pepper and slowly stirred in the flour.

"Peeled potatoes and sliced onions are ready!" Bubbe said. Together Clara and Bubbe dropped the shredded potatoes and onions into the gooey egg yolk. Clara's tummy began to rumble.

Bubbe scooped large spoonfuls of the potato mixture into the pan with hot oil. Sizzle, pop, pop! Clara jumped up and down to the rhythm of the crackling sound, her braids bouncing along to the bubbling beat.

"When the latke begins to turn gold, like the color of your braids, gently slide the spatula underneath and quickly flip it over. There is nothing quite like a crispy latke!" Bubbe said.

Latke, latke, sizzle, pop, pop!
Latke, latke, fry it till it's hot!

Clara and Bubbe sang together as the first latkes were flipped. Mittens hopped down from the counter and nudged Clara's foot.

"You want a taste, you silly kitty?" Clara stepped back from the pan, which was crackling with hot oil. "Bubbe, tell me the story of Chanukah. Tell me the story of the magical oil!"

Bubbe turned the flame down on the stove. "When I was a little girl, my bubbe told me this story as we cooked latkes, just as her bubbe told her and many bubbes and many grandchildren past," she said.

"Long ago, a great temple in Jerusalem was destroyed. Inside the remains of the temple, a teeny-tiny jar of oil was found. The Jews wanted to use the oil to light the menorah and rededicate the temple. However, there was only enough oil to light the menorah for one day."

"Miraculously, the menorah burned for eight days! This holiday is a celebration of that miracle."

Clara's eyes lit up. "That's why we cook latkes for Chanukah! The oil in the pan reminds us of the miracle!"

Bubbe kissed Clara's forehead. "Yes, and this is our tradition! Now, we have a hungry family waiting for our delicious miracle to fill their bellies."

That night, as Clara's eyes gently closed, her dreams took her to the kitchen of a small cottage in a land across the sea, where Bubbe came from.

DING-DONG! The doorbell rang, and Clara jumped out of bed. Mittens chased her down the hall to the front door.

Mom accepted a box from the mail carrier. "Looks like a package from Grammy. It's for you!"

Clara smiled. Opening the box, she found a large red-and-white candy cane with a card attached.

Dearest Clara,

I am looking forward to your visit on Christmas Eve. I will need your help in making our traditional cookies. Grandpa can't wait to decorate the tree with you!

Love,
Grammy

On Christmas Eve, the golden sun was shining brightly. Clara's family began the journey to Grammy and Grandpa's house. Clara caught a glimpse of a shimmering icicle hanging from a tree branch. The icicle was in the shape of Grammy's cookies! She licked her lips. She could already taste the soft, sweet sugar cookie in her mouth.

Clara raced up the wooden steps. Grammy opened the door. "Merry Christmas!" she said with a smile. Brushing her hands on her apron, she gave Clara a warm hug. Grammy smelled sweet, like sugar and butter.

"Let's bake!" Clara said and followed Grammy into the kitchen.

Mittens hopped up onto the kitchen counter. Grammy turned on the mixer, and Clara held on tight to the handle. Mittens peered into the bowl as the butter and sugar churned together to create a sticky, creamy dough. Eggs were cracked, and vanilla was measured with Grammy's favorite teaspoon.

Next came the flour. Each time Clara sprinkled it in, powdery white dust rose up out of the bowl. "Flour cloud!" Clara giggled as some flour tickled Mitten's nose.

Grammy smiled at Clara. "When the dough finally comes together and the flour cloud has settled, it's time to roll it out. We need it nice and flat so the cookie cutter will make a clear imprint of the star. When the dough bakes and begins to turn gold, like the color of your braids, we take them out of the oven. There is nothing quite like a perfect sugar cookie—crispy edges and a soft middle."

Cookie dough, cookie dough, roll it out flat!
Cookie cutter, cookie cutter, pat, pat, pat!

Grammy and Clara sang together as they rolled and pressed the dough. Clara traced her finger around the edges of the star-shaped cookie. "Tell me the story of Christmas! Tell me the story of the magical star!"

Grammy began to place the cookies on a baking sheet. "When I was a little girl, my grammy told me this story as we baked cookies, just as her grammy told her and many grammies and many grandchildren past," she said.

"Long ago, a special king was born in Bethlehem. Three wise men from a distant land heard the news and wanted to bring him gifts. They saw a unique star shining brightly in the sky, and they knew it would guide them on their long journey."

"This miraculous star led them through strong wind and shifting sand, through days and nights until they finally arrived. The three wise men were overjoyed! The star brought them to the king!"

Clara licked some cookie dough off her fingers. "That's why we make these cookies at Christmas! The star shape reminds us of the miracle!"

Grammy hugged Clara. "Yes, and this is our tradition! Now let's share gifts with our family, just as the wise men did many years ago."

That night, as Clara's eyes gently closed, her dreams took her to a different kitchen. She was an old woman with a young boy by her side.

"These holiday treats remind us of two miracles that occurred, miracles we celebrate every December. When I was a little girl, my bubbe told me the Chanukah story as we cooked latkes, and my grammy told me the Christmas story as we baked cookies, just as their grandmothers told them. These traditions were given to me and now I give them to you. This is December's gift."

Latke, latke, sizzle, pop, pop!

Latke, latke, fry it till it's hot!

Bubbe's Latke Recipe

5 large potatoes, peeled and shredded
1 medium onion, finely chopped
3 eggs
1/3 cup flour
pinch of salt and pepper
3/4 cup vegetable oil for frying

Strain grated potatoes and onion through a colander, pressing out excess water.

In a large bowl, whisk eggs, stir in flour, add pinch of salt and pepper. Mix in potatoes and onion.

In a large skillet, heat 1/2 cup of oil. Lower flame and place large tablespoons of mixture into sizzling oil and fry on one side for 3-5 minutes, until golden. Flip over and fry on other side 2-3 minutes. Remove from pan and place on paper towels to drain excess oil. Continue with remaining mixture, adding more oil when necessary. Serve with applesauce.

Cookie dough, cookie dough, roll it out flat!
Cookie cutter, cookie cutter, pat, pat, pat!

Grammy's Sugar Cookie Recipe

3/4 cup butter
1 cup sugar
2 eggs
1 teaspoon vanilla
2 1/2 cups flour
1 teaspoon baking powder
1 teaspoon salt

Cream together butter and sugar. Add eggs and vanilla; beat well. Combine flour, baking powder and salt in separate bowl; mix with butter mixture. Divide dough in half, flatten into disks, wrap in plastic. Refrigerate for at least 1 hour. Roll out dough to 3/8 inch thick. Cut out dough with star cookie cutters. Bake at 400 degrees for 6-8 minutes on a non-stick cookie sheet. Bake until light golden.

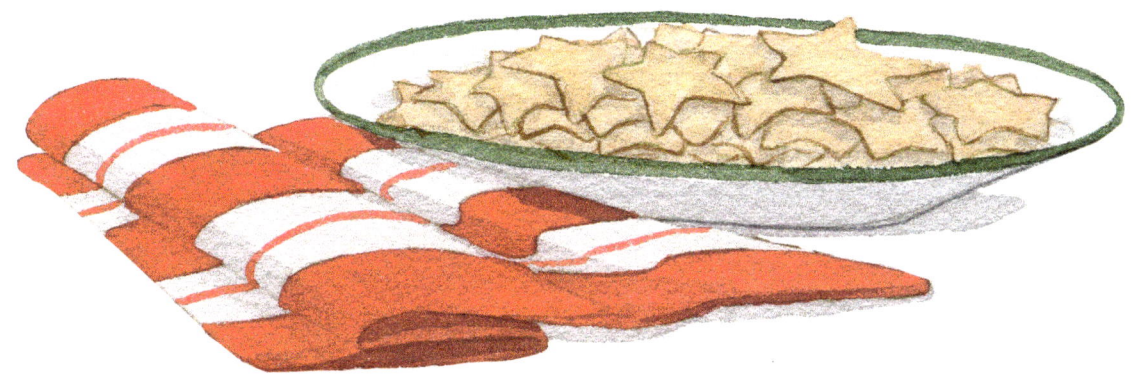

For our families, who gave us the gift of holiday traditions.
-Ashley & Stasie

To the Salsburys, Brumers, and Scotts, for sharing their holiday celebrations.
- Sandra

Text ©2015 by Stasie Bitton
Illustrations ©2015 by Sandra Salsbury

All rights reserved. No part of this book may be used, reproduced, or transmitted in any manner, electronic, graphic, or mechanical without prior written permission from the publisher.

For information please contact: ashleystasie@gmail.com

First Edition
ISBN-13: 978-0-9964783-1-1
ISBN-10: 0-9964783-1-0
Library of Congress Control Number: 2015909127
Stasie Bitton, New York, NY

The interior text of the book was set in Bembo Infant MT Std by Monotype and Lucida Handwriting. The title was set in Tiranti Solid.
The illustrations of this book were painted in watercolor on Arches 140lb coldpress paper.

www.ingramcontent.com/pod-product-compliance
Lightning Source LLC
Chambersburg PA
CBHW061932290426
44113CB00024B/2887